Presented To:

_____

Presented By:

_____

Date:

_____

GOD'S LITTLE INSTRUCTION BOOK FOR GRADUATES

HONOR BOOKS

Inspiration and Motivation for the Season of Life

COOK COMMUNICATIONS MINISTRIES
Colorado Springs, Colorado • Paris, Ontario
KINGSWAY COMMUNICATIONS LTD
Eastbourne, England

Honor Books® is an imprint of
Cook Communications Ministries, Colorado Springs, CO 80918
Cook Communications, Paris, Ontario
Kingsway Communications, Eastbourne, England

GOD'S LITTLE INSTRUCTION BOOK FOR GRADUATES
© 1994, 2003 by HONOR BOOKS
© 2004 by COOK COMMUNICATIONS MINISTRIES

First Printing, 1994
Printed in the UNITED STATES OF AMERICA
5 6 7 8 Printing/Year 08 07 06 05

Unless otherwise noted, Scripture quotations are taken from the *King James Version* of the Bible. Scripture quotations marked NIV is taken from the *Holy Bible, New Internation Version*®. Copyright © 1973, 1978, 1984 International Bible Society. Used by permission of Zondervan. All rights reserved; AMP are taken from the Amplified® Bible, Copyright © 1954, 1958, 1962, 1964, 1965, 1987 by The Lockman Foundation. Used by permission; TLB are taken from The Living Bible, © 1971, Tyndale House Publishers, Wheaton, IL 60189. Used by permission; NASB are taken from the *New American Standard Bible*®, Copyright © The Lockman Foundation 1960, 1962, 1963, 1968, 1971, 1972, 1973, 1975, 1977, 1995. Used by permission.

ISBN 1-56292-670-5

Introduction

God's Little Instruction Book for Graduates is an inspirational collection of quotes and Scriptures that will motivate graduates from high school and college to live a meaningful, productive, and happy life while inspiring them to strive for excellence and character in living.

Some books have quotes and some have Scripture, but we have combined both to provide not just man's insight, but also the wisdom of God. This little book is designed to be fun to read, yet thought-provoking, supplying graduates with godly insight on numerous topics vital to life. You will find familiar and unfamiliar quotes covering subjects such as career achievement, excellence, character and integrity in living, the importance of relationships, and finding real success in life. A Scripture is included after each quote, so you can read what the instruction manual of life, God's Word, has to say about that topic.

This delightful book is basic, practical, and filled with the timeless wisdom of the Bible, covering topics that graduates everywhere can appreciate and learn more about. *God's Little Instruction Book for Graduates* will help graduates reach for excellence as they meet the challenges of the future.

*W*hen you were born, you cried and the world rejoiced. Live your life in such a manner that when you die the world cries and you rejoice.

The memory of the righteous will be a blessing.

PROVERBS 10:7 NIV

*M*any receive advice, only the wise
profit by it.

Pride only breeds quarrels, but wisdom is found in those who take advice.

PROVERBS 13:10 NIV

*E*ven a mosquito doesn't
get a slap on the back
until it starts to work.

Work hard so God can say to you, "Well done." Be a good workman,
one who does not need to be ashamed when God examines your work.

2 TIMOTHY 2:15 TLB

*Y*ou will never make
a more important decision
than the person you marry.

Therefore shall a man leave his father and his mother, and
shall cleave unto his wife: and they shall be one flesh.

GENESIS 2:24

The Bible has a word to describe "safe" sex: it's called marriage.

Marriage should be honored by all, and the marriage bed kept pure,
for God will judge the adulterer and all the sexually immoral.

HEBREWS 13:4 NIV

*N*o horse gets anywhere
until he is harnessed.
No life ever grows great until it is
focused, dedicated, disciplined.

In a race, everyone runs but only one person gets first prize. . . .
To win the contest you must deny yourselves many
things that would keep you from doing your best.

1 CORINTHIANS 9:24-25 TLB

I have never been hurt by anything I didn't say.

Don't talk so much. You keep putting your foot in your mouth. Be sensible and turn off the flow!

PROVERBS 10:19 TLB

*W*e too often love things and use
people, when we should be
using things and loving people.

Be devoted to one another in brotherly love.
Honor one another above yourselves.

ROMANS 12:10 NIV

*O*ne hundred years from now it won't matter if you got that big break, or finally traded up to a Mercedes. . . . It will greatly matter, one hundred years from now, that you made a commitment to Jesus Christ.

What is a man profited, if he shall gain the whole world, and lose his own soul?

MATTHEW 16:26

$\mathcal{S}$uccess is knowing the difference between cornering people and getting them in your corner.

Can two walk together, except they be agreed?

AMOS 3:3

$\mathcal{S}$hoot for the moon.
Even if you miss it you
will land among the stars.

Aim for perfection.
2 CORINTHIANS 13:11 NIV

The secret of success is to
do the common things
uncommonly well.

Seest thou a man diligent in his business? he shall stand
before kings; he shall not stand before mean men.

PROVERBS 22:29

$\mathcal{D}$efinition of status:
buying something you don't
need with money you don't have
to impress people you don't like.

"They do all their deeds to be noticed by men."

MATTHEW 23:5 NASB

I like the dreams of the future better than the history of the past.

Remember ye not the former things, neither consider the things of old. Behold, I will do a new thing.

ISAIAH 43:18-19

*T*he way to get to the top is
to get off your bottom.

How long will you lie down, O sluggard?
When will you arise from your sleep?

PROVERBS 6:9 NASB

You are only what you are when no one is looking.

Not with eyeservice, as menpleasers; but as the servants of Christ, doing the will of God from the heart.

EPHESIANS 6:6

*T*here are times when silence
is golden, other times it is
just plain yellow.

*To everything there is a season . . . a time
to keep silence, and a time to speak.*

ECCLESIASTES 3:1, 7

*K*eep thy shop and thy shop
will keep thee.

He who works his land will have abundant food,
but he who chases fantasies lacks judgement.

PROVERBS 12:11 NIV

*E*very job is a self-portrait
of the person who does it.
Autograph your work with excellence.

Daniel was preferred above the presidents and princes,
because an excellent spirit was in him.

DANIEL 6:3

The best things in life are *not* free.

Ye know that ye were not redeemed with corruptible things,
as silver and gold . . . but with the precious blood of Christ,
as of a lamb without blemish and without spot.

1 PETER 1:18-19

You can lead a boy to college, but you cannot make him think.

It is senseless to pay tuition to educate a rebel who has no heart for truth.

PROVERBS 17:16 TLB

*I*f a man cannot be a Christian in the place where he is, he cannot be a Christian anywhere.

Don't work hard only when your master is watching and then shirk when he isn't looking; work hard and with gladness all the time, as though working for Christ, doing the will of God with all your hearts.

EPHESIANS 6:6-7 TLB

*D*on't ask God for what you think is good; ask him for what He thinks is good for you.

After this manner therefore pray ye. . . . Thy kingdom come.
Thy will be done in earth, as it is in heaven.

MATTHEW 6:9-10

*O*pportunities are seldom labeled.

Seek, and ye shall find; knock, and it shall be opened unto you.

MATTHEW 7:7

*T*he wise does at once what the fool does at last.

He that gathereth in summer is a wise son: but he that sleepeth in harvest is a son that causeth shame.

PROVERBS 10:5

*N*othing great was ever achieved without enthusiasm.

The joy of the LORD is your strength.

NEHEMIAH 8:10

*T*rust in yourself and you are doomed to disappointment. . . . But trust in God, and you are never to be confounded in time or eternity.

It is better to take refuge in the LORD than to trust in man.

PSALM 118:8 NIV

$\mathcal{D}$on't be discouraged;
everyone who got where he is,
started where he was.

Though your beginning was insignificant,
Yet your end will increase greatly.

JOB 8:7 NASB

*M*aturity doesn't come
with age; it comes with
acceptance of responsibility.

When I was a child, I spake as a child, I understood as a child, I thought
as a child: but when I became a man, I put away childish things.

1 CORINTHIANS 13:11

*T*he man who wins may have
been counted out several times,
but he didn't hear the referee.

Though a righteous man falls seven times, he rises again.

PROVERBS 24:16 NIV

*T*he happiest people
don't necessarily have the
best of everything. They just
make the best of everything.

I have learned, in whatsoever state I am, therewith to be content. . . .
I can do all things through Christ which strengtheneth me.

PHILIPPIANS 4:11, 13

$\mathcal{K}$eep company with good men and good men you will imitate.

Iron sharpeneth iron; so a man sharpeneth the countenance of his friend.

PROVERBS 27:17

$\mathcal{L}$earn by experience—
preferably other people's.

All these things happened to them as examples—as object
lessons to us—to warn us against doing the same things.

1 CORINTHIANS 10:11 TLB

*I*t is not what a man does that determines whether his work is sacred or secular, it is why he does it.

Whatever you do, work at it with all your heart, as working for the Lord, not for men. . . . It is the Lord Christ you are serving.

COLOSSIANS 3:23-24 NIV

*I*t's not hard to make decisions when you know what your values are.

Daniel purposed in his heart that he would not defile himself.

DANIEL 1:8

*C*onquer yourself rather
than the world.

Encourage the young men to be self-controlled.

TITUS 2:6 NIV

I am only one; but still I am one. I cannot do everything, but still I can do something; I will not refuse to do the something I can do.

Under his [Christ's] *direction the whole body is fitted together perfectly, and each part in its own special way helps the other parts.*

EPHESIANS 4:16 TLB

*P*oliteness goes far,
yet costs nothing.

A kind man benefits himself.

PROVERBS 11:17 NIV

*W*e should behave to our friends
as we would wish our friends
to behave to us.

As ye would that men should do to you, do ye also to them likewise.

LUKE 6:31

The end must justify the means.

The just man walketh in his integrity:
his children are blessed after him.

PROVERBS 20:7

*C*haracter is what you
are in the dark.

The integrity of the upright shall guide them.

PROVERBS 11:3

*A*dversity causes some men to break; others to break records.

If thou faint in the day of adversity, thy strength is small.

PROVERBS 24:10

To love what you do and feel
that it matters—how could
anything be more fun?

My heart rejoiced in all my labour.

ECCLESIASTES 2:10

A man who wants to
lead the orchestra must
turn his back on the crowd.

Come out from among them, and be ye separate, saith the Lord,
and touch not the unclean thing; and I will receive you.

2 CORINTHIANS 6:17

*M*en are alike in their promises.
It is only in their deeds
that they differ.

Many a man claims to have unfailing love,
but a faithful man who can find?

PROVERBS 20:6 NIV

$\mathcal{D}$on't cross your bridges until you get to them. We spend our lives defeating ourselves crossing bridges we never get to.

"Don't be anxious about tomorrow. God will take care of your tomorrow too. Live one day at a time."

MATTHEW 6:34 TLB

*H*e that has learned to obey will know how to command.

The wise in heart accept commands,
but a chattering fool comes to ruin.

PROVERBS 10:8 NIV

*Y*ou must have long-range goals to keep you from being frustrated by short-range failures.

Let us fix our eyes on Jesus, the author and perfecter of our faith, who for the joy set before him endured the cross, scorning its shame, and sat down at the right hand of the throne of God.

HEBREWS 12:2

Clear your mind of can't.

I can do all things through Christ which strengtheneth me.

PHILIPPIANS 4:13

*T*he future belongs to those
who believe in the beauty
of their dreams.

"Anything is possible if you have faith."

MARK 9:23 TLB

*T*he future belongs to those
who see possibilities before
they become obvious.

The vision is yet for an appointed time . . .
it will surely come, it will not tarry.

HABAKKUK 2:3

When I was a young man I observed that nine out of ten things I did were failures. I didn't want to be a failure, so I did ten times more work.

The sluggard craves and gets nothing, but the desires of the diligent are fully satisfied.

PROVERBS 13:4

$\mathscr{D}$o not wait for extraordinary
circumstances to do good;
try to use ordinary situations.

Make the most of every opportunity.

COLOSSIANS 4:5 NIV

*J*umping to conclusions is not
half as good an exercise
as digging for facts.

*Study to show thyself approved unto God, a workman that
needeth not to be ashamed, rightly dividing the word of truth.*

2 TIMOTHY 2:15

*T*he most valuable of all talents
is that of never using
two words when one will do.

In the multitude of words there wanteth not sin:
but he that refraineth his lips is wise.

PROVERBS 10:19

$\mathscr{L}$aziness is often mistaken for patience.

Let us lay aside every weight, and the sin which doth so easily beset us, and let us run with patience the race that is set before us.

HEBREWS 12:1

*O*ne-half the trouble of this life can be traced to saying yes too quick, and not saying no soon enough.

Seest thou a man that is hasty in his words?
There is more hope of a fool than of him.

PROVERBS 29:20

I would rather fail in the cause
that someday will triumph
than triumph in a cause
that someday will fail.

Thanks be unto God, which always causeth us to triumph in Christ.

2 CORINTHIANS 2:14

*C*arve your name on hearts
and not on marble.

The only letter I need is you yourselves! They can see that you are a letter
from Christ written by us . . . not one carved on stone, but in human hearts.

2 CORINTHIANS 3:2-3 TLB

A knowledge of the Bible
without a college course is more
valuable than a college course
without the Bible.

All scripture is given by inspiration of God, and is profitable for doctrine,
for reproof, for correction, for instruction in righteousness: that the man
of God may be perfect, thoroughly furnished unto all good works.

2 TIMOTHY 3:16-17

*L*ittle minds are tamed and subdued by misfortune; but great minds rise above them.

A just man falleth seven times, and riseth up again.

PROVERBS 24:16

*T*here is no poverty that
can overtake dilligence.

He becometh poor that dealeth with a slack hand:
but the hand of the diligent maketh rich.

PROVERBS 10:4

*N*ever despair; but if you do,
work on in despair.

As for you, be strong and do not give up, for your work will be rewarded.

2 CHRONICLES 15:7 NIV

You can accomplish more
in one hour with God than
one lifetime without him.

With God all things are possible.

MATTHEW 19:26

*I*f you don't stand for something
you'll fall for anything!

If you do not stand firm in your faith, you will not stand at all.

ISAIAH 7:9 NIV

*T*he difference between ordinary and extraordinary is that little extra.

Whatever you do, do well.

ECCLESIASTES 9:10 TLB

*M*an cannot discover new oceans
unless he has the courage
to lose sight of the shore.

Peter got out of the boat, and walked on the water and came toward Jesus.

MATTHEW 14:29 NASB

*E*very man is enthusiastic at times. One man has enthusiasm for thirty minutes, another has it for thirty days— but it is the man that has it for thirty years who makes a success in life.

Let us run with perseverance the race marked out for us.

HEBREWS 12:1 NIV

*P*erseverance is a great element of success; if you only knock long enough and loud enough at the gate you are sure to wake up somebody.

Ask, and it shall be given you; seek, and ye shall find; knock, and it shall be opened unto you.

LUKE 11:9

*C*onsider the postage stamp:
its usefulness consists in the ability
to stick to one thing till it gets there.

I have fought a good fight, I have finished my course, I have kept the faith.

2 TIMOTHY 4:7

It needs more skill than I can tell to play the second fiddle well.

He that is greatest among you shall be your servant.

MATTHEW 23:11

A man never discloses his own
character so clearly as when
he describes another's.

A good man out of the good treasure of the heart bringeth forth good things;
and an evil man out of the evil treasure bringeth forth evil things.

MATTHEW 12:35

*T*he greatest use of life is to spend it for something that will outlast it.

"Store up for yourselves treasures in heaven, where moth and rust do not destroy, and where thieves do not break in and steal."

MATTHEW 6:20 NIV

*E*very man's work, whether it be
literature, or music, or pictures,
or architecture, or anything else,
is always a portrait of himself.

As in water face reflects face, so the heart of man reflects man.

PROVERBS 27:19 NASB

*W*hat we do on some great occasion
will probably depend on what
we already are; and what we are
will be the result of previous
years of self-discipline.

I keep under my body, and bring it into submission.

1 CORINTHIANS 9:27

*O*ur deeds determine us, as much as we determine our deeds.

Even a child is known by his actions,
by whether his conduct is pure and right.

PROVERBS 20:11 NIV

What you do speaks so loud that I cannot hear what you say.

Show me your faith without deeds, and
I will show you my faith by what I do.

JAMES 2:18 NIV

*A*ll virtue is summed up in dealing justly.

He hath shewed thee, O man, what is good; and
what doth the LORD require of thee, but to do justly,
and to love mercy, and to walk humbly with thy God?

MICAH 6:8

*N*o matter what a man's past
may have been,
his future is spotless.

Forgetting those things which are behind, and
reaching forth unto those things which are before.

PHILIPPIANS 3:13

One of life's great rules is this:
the more you give,
the more you get.

The liberal soul shall be made fat: and he that
watereth shall be watered also himself.

PROVERBS 11:24-25

*E*verything comes to him
who hustles while he waits.

*We do not want you to become lazy, but to imitate those who
through faith and patience inherit what has been promised.*

HEBREWS 6:12 NIV

A well-trained memory is one that permits you to forget everything that isn't worth remembering.

Whatsoever things are true, whatsoever things are honest, whatsoever things are just . . . if there be any virtue, and if there be any praise, think on these things.

PHILIPPIANS 4:8

$\mathcal{D}$efeat is not the worst of failures.
Not to have tried is
the true failure.

Be strong and of a good courage; be not afraid, neither be thou dismayed:
for the LORD thy God is with thee whithersoever thou goest.

JOSHUA 1:9

*U*nless you try to do something
beyond what you have
already mastered,
you will never grow.

*I am still not all I should be, but I am bringing all my energies to
bear on this one thing . . . I strain to reach the end of the race. . . .*

PHILIPPIANS 3:13-14 TLB

I don't know the secret to
success but the key to failure
is to try to please everyone.

Am I now trying to win the approval of man or of God?

GALATIANS 1:10 NIV

*K*ites rise highest against
the wind, not with it.

When the way is rough, your patience has a chance to grow.
So let it grow, and don't try to squirm out of your problems.

JAMES 1:3-4 TLB

*T*he secret of success is to be like a duck—smooth and unruffled on top, but paddling furiously underneath.

I laboured more abundantly than they all: yet not I,
but the grace of God which was with me.

1 CORINTHIANS 15:10

*T*he cheerful man will do more in
the same time, will do it better,
will preserve it longer,
than the sad or sullen.

*When a man is gloomy, everything seems to go wrong;
when he is cheerful, everything seems right!*

PROVERBS 15:15 TLB

*M*oney is a good servant
but a bad master.

The rich ruleth over the poor, and the borrower is servant to the lender.

PROVERBS 22:7

*N*o plan is worth the paper
it is printed on unless it
starts you doing something.

Be ye doers of the word, and not hearers only, deceiving your own selves.

JAMES 1:22

*L*ife is a coin. You can spend
it any way you wish, but
you can spend it only once.

As is it appointed unto men once to die, but after this the judgment.

HEBREWS 9:27 NIV

*O*nly passions, great passions,
can elevate the soul
to great things.

Fervent in spirit; serving the Lord.

ROMANS 12:11

$\mathcal{F}$ailures want pleasing methods, successes want pleasing results.

No discipline seems pleasant at the time, but painful.
Later on, however, it produces a harvest of righteousness
and peace for those who have been trained by it.

HEBREWS 12:11 NIV

*O*nce a word has been
allowed to escape,
it cannot be recalled.

*Let no corrupt communication proceed out of your mouth, but that which
is good to the use of edifying, that it may minister grace unto the hearers.*

EPHESIANS 4:29

*M*ost of the things worth doing
in the world had been declared
impossible before they were done.

With God all things are possible.

MATTHEW 19:26

*O*bstacles are those frightful things you see when you take your eyes off the goal.

So Peter . . . walked on the water toward Jesus. But when he looked around at the high waves, he was terrified and began to sink.

MATTHEW 14:29-30 TLB

A good reputation is more
valuable than money.

A good name is rather to be chosen than great riches.

PROVERBS 22:1

*A*n error doesn't become a mistake
until you refuse to correct it.

*He who heeds discipline shows the way to life, but
whoever ignores correction leads others astray.*

PROVERBS 10:17 NIV

*H*ating people is like
burning down your own
house to get rid of a rat.

*If ye bite and devour one another, take heed
that ye be not consumed one of another.*

GALATIANS 5:15

*L*aughter is the sun
that drives winter
from the human face.

A merry heart maketh a cheerful countenance:
but by sorrow of the heart the spirit is broken.

PROVERBS 15:13

*G*ood nature begets smiles,
smiles beget friends, and
friends are better than a fortune.

The light in the eyes [of him whose heart is joyful] rejoices the heart of others.

PROVERBS 15:30 AMP

*N*o person was ever honored
for what he received.
Honor has been the
reward for what he gave.

The righteous give without sparing.

PROVERBS 21:26 NIV

*G*ood words are worth
much and cost little.

A word fitly spoken is like apples of gold in pictures of silver.

PROVERBS 25:11

*T*his world belongs to the man
who is wise enough to change
his mind in the presence of facts.

Whoever heeds correction gains understanding.

PROVERBS 15:32 NIV

*B*lessed is the man who is too busy to worry in the daytime and too sleepy to worry at night.

The sleep of a labouring man is sweet.

ECCLESIASTES 5:12

*E*very calling is great
when greatly pursued.

*I press toward the mark for the prize of
the high calling of God in Christ Jesus.*

PHILIPPIANS 3:14

*T*reat everybody alike, no matter from what station in life he comes. . . . Really great men and women are those who are natural, frank, and honest with everyone with whom they come into contact.

Don't show favoritism

JAMES 2:1 NIV

'*T*is better to be alone,
than in bad company.

Do not be misled: "Bad company corrupts good character."

1 CORINTHIANS 15:33 NIV

*T*he rotten apple spoils his companion.

He that walketh with wise men shall be wise:

but a companion of fools shall be destroyed.

PROVERBS 13:20

*P*atience is bitter but its fruit is sweet.

Ye have need of patience, that, after ye have done the will of God, ye might receive the promise.

HEBREWS 10:36

*T*he greedy search for money or success will almost always lead men into unhappiness. Why? Because that kind of life makes them depend upon things outside themselves.

Let your character be free from the love of money, being
content with what you have; for He Himself has said,
"I will never desert you nor will I ever forsake you."

HEBREWS 13:5 NASB

*N*ot only to say the right thing in the right place, but far more difficult, to leave unsaid the wrong thing at the tempting moment.

Self-control means controlling the tongue!
A quick retort can ruin everything.

PROVERBS 13:3 TLB

*S*chool seeks to get you
ready for examination;
life gives the finals.

Examine yourselves to see whether you are in the faith; test yourselves.

2 CORINTHIANS 13:5 NIV

$\mathscr{D}$iligence is the mother
of good fortune.

The plans of the diligent lead to profit.

PROVERBS 21:5 NIV

$\mathcal{T}$he road to success is dotted
with many tempting
parking places.

Let us lay aside every weight, and the sin which doth so easily beset us,
and let us run with patience the race that is set before us.

HEBREWS 12:1

*W*hen you are laboring for others let it be with the same zeal as if it were for yourself.

Each of you should look not only to your own interests, but also to the interests of others.

PHILIPPIANS 2:4 NIV

The Bible knows nothing
of a hierarchy of labor.
No work is degrading.
If it ought to be done,
then it is good work.

To rejoice in his labour; this is the gift of God.

ECCLESIASTES 5:19

$\mathcal{T}$he ripest peach is
the highest on the tree.

Let us not become weary in doing good, for at the proper
time we will reap a harvest if we do not give up.

GALATIANS 6:9 NIV

When you do the things you have to do
when you have to do them,
the day will come when you can do
the things you want to do
when you want to do them.

He becometh poor that dealeth with a slack hand:
but the hand of the diligent maketh rich.

PROVERBS 10:4

A man without mirth is
like a wagon without springs,
he is jolted disagreeably
by every pebble in the road.

A merry heart doeth good like a medicine:
but a broken spirit drieth the bones.

PROVERBS 17:22

*T*he 2 most important words:
"thank you."
The most important word: "we."
The least important word: "I."

Don't be selfish. . . . Be humble, thinking of others as better than yourself.

PHILIPPIANS 2:3 TLB

$\mathcal{H}$ere's the key of success
and the key to failure:
we become what we think about.

To be carnally minded is death; but to be
spiritually minded is life and peace.

ROMANS 8:6 KJV

*A*lways bear in mind that
your own resolution to success
is more important than
any other one thing.

*The Lord GOD will help me; therefore shall I not be confounded: therefore
have I set my face like a flint, and I know that I shall not be ashamed.*

ISAIAH 50:7

*T*riumph is just "umph"
added to try.

Whatsoever thy hand findeth to do, do it with thy might.

ECCLESIASTES 9:10

A goal properly set is
halfway reached.

The LORD answered me, and said, Write the vision, and
make it plain upon tables, that he may run that readeth it.

HABAKKUK 2:2

I think the one lesson I have
learned is that there is
no substitute for
paying attention.

We ought to give the more earnest heed to the things which
we have heard, lest at any time we should let them slip.

HEBREWS 2:1

A good listener is not only
popular everywhere, but after
a while he knows something.

The ear that heareth the reproof of life abideth among the wise.

PROVERBS 15:31

*S*uccess is never final;
failure is never fatal;
it is courage that counts.

*Be of good courage, and he shall strengthen
your heart, all ye that hope in the LORD.*

PSALM 31:24

I count him braver who overcomes
his desires than him who
conquers his enemies; for the
hardest victory is the victory over self.

I beat my body and make it my slave.

1 CORINTHIANS 9:27 NIV

*V*ision is the world's most desperate need. There are no hopeless situations, only people who think hopelessly.

Where there is no vision, the people perish.

PROVERBS 29:18

"*The* Supervisor's Prayer"
Lord when I am wrong, make me willing
to change; when I am right, make me
easy to live with. So strengthen me
that the power of my example will
far exceed the authority of my rank.

To offer ourselves as a model for you, that you might follow our example.

2 THESSALONIANS 3:9 NASB

*G*ive me a task too big, too hard
for human hands, then I shall
come at length to lean on thee,
and leaning, find my strength.

*Trust in the LORD with all your heart
and lean not on your own understanding.*

PROVERBS 3:5 NIV

*T*he most important single ingredient
in the formula of success is
knowing how to get along with people.

See that no one pays back evil for evil, but always
try to do good to each other and to everyone else.

1 THESSALONIANS 5:15 TLB

*E*veryone thinks of changing
the world, but no one
thinks of changing himself.

*"Unless you change and become like little children
you will never enter the kingdom of heaven."*

MATTHEW 18:3 NIV

*P*rayer is an invisible tool
which is wielded in
a visible world.

The weapons of our warfare are not carnal, but mighty
through God to the pulling down of strong holds.

2 CORINTHIANS 10:4

*M*oney is like an arm or leg:
use it or lose it.

"To him who has will more be given . . . and he will have great plenty;
but from him who has not, even the little he has will be taken away."

MATTHEW 13:12 TLB

*L*et us not say, every man is the
architect of his own fortune;
but let us say, every man is
the architect of his own character.

Till I die I will not remove mine integrity from me. My righteousness I hold fast, and will not let it go: my heart shall not reproach me so long as I live.

JOB 27:5-6

*I*t is impossible for that man
to despair who remembers
that his helper is omnipotent.

I will lift up my eyes to the mountains; from whence shall my help come?
My help comes from the LORD, who made heaven and earth.

PSALM 12:1-2 NASB

The price of success is hard work, dedication to the job at hand, and determination that whether we win or lose, we have applied the best of ourselves to the task at hand.

Whatsoever ye do, do it heartily, as to the Lord, and not unto men.

COLOSSIANS 3:23

*T*hose that have done nothing in life
are not qualified to be judge
of those that have done little.

Judge not, and ye shall not be judged:
condemn not, and ye shall not be condemned.

LUKE 6:37

*P*eople, places, and things were
never meant to give us life.
God alone is the author
of a fulfilling life.

I am come that they might have life, and
that they might have it more abundantly.

JOHN 10:10

Common Courtesies for Graduates

"Just as you want people to treat you, treat them in the same way."

LUKE 6:31 NASB

*A*lways say thank-you,
excuse me, and please.

*A*lways knock and
ask permission before
entering someone's room.

Don't put your feet up
on the furniture.
Feet do not enhance the
look of the desk or the table.

*A*lways RSVP promptly to every invitation you receive.

Return anything borrowed on time,
and in good condition.

*B*e on time for appointments;
leave on time too, for nothing
is more boring than someone
who overstays his welcome.

When you dial a wrong number, say,
"I'm sorry, excuse me"—instead of
slamming down the receiver
in the other person's ear.

$\mathcal{N}$ever cut in line.

$\mathcal{S}$how respect to anyone
in authority.

*D*rive your car carefully,
not only out of consideration
for others but also to save lives.

*L*earn how to pay compliments.
Start with the members of your family,
and you will find it will become easier
later in life to compliment others.
It's a great asset.

Acknowledgements

Syrus (6), Dr. Eugene Swearingen (8,17,19), Gary Smalley & John Trent (9,145), Harry Emerson Fosdick (10,103), Calvin Coolidge (11,106), David Shibley (13), Bill Copeland (14), Les Brown (15), John D. Rockefeller Jr. (16), Thomas Jefferson (18,59), Robert C. Edward (20), Ed Cole (21,33,139), Benjamin Franklin (22,113), Kin Hubbard (25), Henry Ward Beecher (26,124), John A. Shedd (28), Ralph Waldo Emerson (30,81), Dwight L. Moody (31,45), H. E. Jansen (34), A. W. Tozer (38), Roy Disney (39), Descartes (40), Helen Keller (41), Seneca (42), Aristotle (43,82,133), Matthew Prior (44), William A. Ward (46), Katherine Graham (47), Moliere (49), Bob Bales (50), Solon (51), Charles C. Noble (52), Samuel Johnson (53,144), Eleanor Roosevelt (54), John Sculley (55), George Bernard Shaw (56), Johann Paul Friedrich Richter (57,76), Woodrow Wilson (62), Charles H. Spurgeon (63), William Lyon Phelps (64), Washington Irving (65), Terence (67), Henry Wadsworth Longfellow (73), Josh Billings (74), William James (77), Samuel Butler (78), H. P. Liddon (79), George Elliot (80), John R. Rice (83), William H. Danforth (84,94,111), Thomas A. Edison (85), Battista (86), George Edward Woodberry (87), Ronald E. Osborn (88), Bill Cosby (89), Winston Churchill (90,132), Thomas Carlyle (92), Dominique Bouhours (93), Lillian Dickson (95), Denis Diderot (96), Earl Nightingale (97,126), Horace (98), Louis D. Brandeis (99), Hannah More (100), Publilius Syrus (101), Orlando A. Battista (102), Victor Hugo (104), David Dunn (105), George Herbert (107), Roy L. Smith (108), Phil Marquart (109), Oliver Wendell Holmes (110), George Washington (112), Andre Maurois (115), George Sala (116), Say (117), Cervantes (118), Ben Patterson (121), James Whitcomb Riley (122), Zig Ziglar (123,129), Builder (125), Abraham Lincoln (127), Diane Sawyer (130), Wilson Mizner (131), Winifred Newman (134), Pauline H. Peters (135), Witt Fowler (136), Theodore Roosevelt (137), Leo Tolstoy (138), Henry Ford (140), George Dana Boardman (141), Jeremy Taylor (142), Vince Lombardi (143).

Additional copies of this and other titles
from Honor Books are available from your local bookseller.

God's Little Instruction Book
God's Little Instruction Book for Mothers
God's Little Instruction Book for Couples
God's Little Instruction Book for Men
God's Little Instruction Book for Teachers
God's Little Instruction Book for Teens
God's Little Instruction Book for Women
God's Little Instruction Book for African Americans

If you have enjoyed this book, or if it has had an impact on your life,
we would like to hear from you.

Please contact us at:

HONOR BOOKS
Cook Communications Ministries, Dept. 201
4050 Lee Vance View
Colorado Springs, CO 80918
Or visit our Web site:
www.cookministries.com

HONOR HB BOOKS

Inspiration and Motivation for the Season of Life